Eunice V. Boudinot

Patriotic Poems

Eunice V. Boudinot

Patriotic Poems

ISBN/EAN: 9783337307097

Printed in Europe, USA, Canada, Australia, Japan

Cover: Foto ©Thomas Meinert / pixelio.de

More available books at **www.hansebooks.com**

PATRIOTIC POEMS

—BY—

MRS. EUNICE V. BOUDINOT.

AN IOWA BOOK FOR PATRIOTIC PEOPLE.

PRICE $1.00.

SOLD ONLY BY SUBSCRIPTION.

DES MOINES, IOWA:
STATE REGISTER PRINTING HOUSE.
1898.

TO ALL SOLDIERS

EVERYWHERE, ESPECIALLY THOSE OF MY NATIVE STATE, IOWA, CROCKER'S IOWA OLD BRIGADE, CO. B, FIFTEENTH IOWA INFANTRY, TO WHICH MY HUSBAND WM. A. BOUDINOT BELONGED AND TO HIS MEMORY; ALSO FIRST REGIMENT U. S. CAVALRY, FORTY-NINTH, FIFTIETH, FIFTY-FIRST AND FIFTY-SECOND IOWA INFANTRY VOLUNTEERS, BEVER'S BATTERY No. 5, AND BURLINGTON BATTERY No. 6, LIGHT ARTILLERY, AND BRANDT'S IOWA IMMUNES, IS THIS VOLUME RESPECTFULLY DEDICATED BY THE AUTHOR.

TABLE OF CONTENTS.

	PAGE
Introductory	5
Columbia, the Land of the Free	7
Breaking Camp	9
Our Boys are gone	11
My Title	14
Dewey's Feat	15
Cardenas Bay	16
Bottling of Cervera's Fleet	18
Hobson	19
Guantanamo	21
La Quasima	21
Santiago	22
El Caney Heroes	23
Sampson's Victory	25
Manzanillo	25
Rejoicings	26
Summary	26
Our Queen—a tribute to Miss Gould	29
Peace	30
History Repeats Itself	31
Our Colored Immunes	31
Our 52d Iowa Boys	34
Ghosts	36
Welcome Home 50th Iowa	43
Cedar Rapids	45
Song—Helen Gould	46
Naval Parade	47
Re-united	51
Captain Goodrell	59
Peace Jubilee	61

	PAGE
To Our Boys of the 49th and 51st Iowa	103
Equal to any Occasion	106
Aunt Beckey Young	107
Where's My Papa?	110
Sanitary Commission	112
Iowa's Soldier Girl	114
Osborne Deignan's Welcome Home	116
Admonition	119
Only a Flirtation	120
Love	122
Noontime Musings	123
Tribute to the Soldier's Friend	126
In Conclusion	127

INTRODUCTORY.

A dispatch from Des Moines says: "Mrs. E. V. Boudinot, a country school teacher in Linn County, whose postoffice is Western College, has started a movement which is likely to result in giving the soldier boys a little pocket pamphlet of patriotic songs. Mrs. Boudinot is a soldier's widow, and as a teacher she had received a copy of the Memorial Day leaflet, issued by the state department of education. She came all the way to Des Moines last Saturday to say good by to the boys of the Cedar Rapids company, many of whom she had known from childhood, and some of whom had been her pupils. It occurred to her that she would like to give the boys some of the Memorial Day leaflets, which contain many patriotic songs, Bob Cousins' famous speech on the Maine, and some other patriotic speeches. So she called on Superintendent Barrett and when her purpose was made known he gave her seventy-five copies of the leaflet for the boys. In the afternoon she came back and reported that they were perfectly delighted to receive these little pamphlets and would carry them with care and pride to the front. This suggested the propriety of giving every Iowa soldier a little collection of patriotic songs, printed on good strong paper, with the flag on the cover. Americans have been reproached for not knowing their own national songs and probably not one person in fifty can repeat "The Star Spangled Banner" or "America." If the boys had these little song books they would soon learn the songs and the singing would be more general than it is. They would surely appreciate and prize such a gift, and it would not be expensive. It is likely that some way will be found to have the songs printed and distributed."

The foregoing is quoted from the Cedar Rapids Daily *Republican* of June 1, 1898.

It has, through appreciation shown, given me courage to write and have published a few little poems.

If any soldier, on reading these verses, shall feel renewed courage, and be brought into closer sympathy with his Heavenly Father, who rules the destinies of nations, allotting to them according to their deserts, I shall feel myself well repaid for the little it is in my power to do to cheer them.

Money I have not, and as for getting a position as nurse, I have thought of that, and would gladly have gone to the front to do all I could, but there seemed to be a very great difficulty in the way of getting an appointment. But, "Whatsoever thy hands find to do, do with thy might," is an injunction that has carried weight with me, especially in this case, for my hands were occupied with school teaching, and, incidentally, teaching patriotism and appreciation for the sufferings and sacrifices of those noble patriots of our nation who have, at different times, laid life with all its ambition, promise of joy and happiness, upon the shrine of duty to step forth at country's bidding, to face all dangers, inconveniences and hardships for the good of their country. In this war the motive is doubly to be commended, as our boys are fighting, enduring hardships, fatigues and risks of all kinds for the benefit of a race of people not allied to us by bond of blood, but who, nevertheless, have our sympathies for the determined resistance they have offered to the tyranny of that perjured nation, Spain, from whose shackles they have so often tried to free themselves.

"God moves in a mysterious way his wonders to perform;
He plants his footsteps in the sea and rides upon the storm."

Wishing you all happiness, in both this and the world to come, I am, devotedly,

EUNICE V. BOUDINOT, *Author*.

Western College, Linn Co., Iowa.

P. S. Most of the proceeds of the sale of this book I shall use for the benefit of our soldier boys in paying the expense of sending copies to those who are to remain in the service.

Columbia, the Land of the Free . . .

Columbia! Columbia! thou land of the free,
The oppressed of all nations look upward toward thee;
The war cloud has gathered, how darkly it lowers,
But thou'lt be triumphant in spite of the "powers,"
For God is thine ally; in Him thou canst trust!
He can humble and crumble all nations to dust.

If from thy proud height thou hadst stooped to come down
To "compromise," barter in souls! with what frown
Would Jehovah have rebuked thee: nor have strengthened thine arm;
Nor allowed of thy glory; but instead have sent harm
To humble and crush thee, Columbia, to earth,
For thou boasteth that here 'tis Fair Freedom had birth.

Proud boast! Prove it true, men of valor and might.
Men of wealth and of honor, come forward and fight.
For the right and for vengeance, which is mine, saith the Lord!
And I will repay! Can you doubt, doubt His word?

The pages of history are rife with this fact,
That, martyrs and heroes come forward and act;
They, the means, in God's hands, for man's
　　progress have given
Their lives, and their all. They shall find them
　　in Heaven.

If "God take account of the sparrows that fall,"
These, His heroes, are watched and accounted
　　for, all!
Not one but God sees! and so loves day by day,
That He gave His own Son to open the way
For man's freedom and progress. And thus it
　　is given
That if life is lost here, it is gained in God's
　　Heaven.

Breaking Camp . . .

"Good bye," we hear, "God bless you!"
"Good bye," returns again.
"Ah yes! we're going to Cuba
To fight, and not in vain."

"Cuba shall be free at last,"
"We'll not forget the Maine."
"God speed you, boys! God speed you!"
The mothers say again.

"But remember, boys, remember,
To write to us at home!
We'll wait with eager longing
The letters, 'till they come!"

"You have gone at country's bidding,
And under Heaven's wide dome,
No one could do more nobly,
Than go as you have gone."

"Keep always this in mind, boys,
Your're fighting for the right!
For your country's honor, boys,
To show the world her might."

"Keep clean and pure your records
Through every day and night,
Remember, God is everywhere!
You're always in His sight!"

"Our prayers are offered for you,
Every minute of each day."
"I need them!" "Yes, and I, too!"
We hear young voices say.

"A last good bye!" "We're going now!"
"Ah yes! We're off today!"
"Well, then, God bless and keep you, boys,
While you are far away."

"My boy is gone! Oh, God in heaven!
How can I give him up?
He was my life! my very all!
Oh! bitter is this cup!"

"But God in Heaven can keep him!
My boy! My hero brave!
If here no more I see him,
We shall meet beyond the grave!"

"For God's ways are mysterious,
His wonders to perform,
He plants his footsteps in the sea
And rides the upon storm."

Our Boys are Gone . . .

Our boys left Sunday—youth, valor and might—
For Phillippine isles, far away;
Of each home, the treasure, life, joy and light,
Our Iowa boys, gone to stay
A long two years, in those far topic seas.
Colonel Loper, look after them, pray!

The boys, our jewels, our brightest and best,
We give with free, generous hand
To God, our country, to mankind oppressed
By Spain, in that far distant land.
Two years! that our flag may float over those seas.
Colonel Loper, pray, to them be kind.

They've just left their homes, these dear children
 of ours,
So young now, so buoyant, so brave!
They seem more adapted to gathering flowers
Than glory, which "leads to the grave."
Two years, that our flag may float over those seas,
Colonel Loper, attention we crave.

When they left Camp McKinley, 'twas rainy,
 damp;
What cared we for weather that day?
We waded through water and mud to the camp
To bid them "God speed" on their way.
In each face, firm purpose flamed out as a lamp.
Colonel Loper, we trust you, we say.

The fathers were there, who had fought in years
 past,
And gallantly offered their all
In the late civil war. We hoped 'twas the last
To which we should ever have call.
But they're gone, yes, they're gone, for two,
 whole, long years.
Colonel Loper, look after them all.

The mothers came out there to see the boys go,
They tried to be cheerful and brave;
But in spite of effort they could not be so,
Then full vent to feelings they gave,
As clasped in son's arms for the last time for
 years.
Colonel Loper, "please take care of Dave."

The sisters came out, too, defying the rain,
All looking their sweetest and best,
Waved kerchiefs, flags, hands, choked back sobs,
 all in vain,
Their brothers are off for the West,
To be gone two years, on that far away main,
Colonel Loper, will see to the rest.

Young brothers were there, perched on telegraph
   poles,
To see the boys march as they passed.
They squeezed back their tears, for they have
   manly souls.
Bound they'd not cry, even at last.
"But if we were old enough we'd go along.
With Loper and boys we'd cling fast."

The sweethearts, so timid, were on the grounds,
   too.
Their soft eyes full, suffused with tears,
One last fond farewell, a sad lingering adieu,
"Oh, I'll not see my hero for years!
If he should be wounded, what then will I do?"
"Faith in Loper quiets my fears."

As for Loper himself, God will care for him,
And help him take care of the boys;
May faith in God lead, may his eyes ne'er grow
   dim.
May he have many years full of joys,
When conquering heroes come back home again,
Saying, "Loper took care of us boys."

My Title . . . .

American! That is my name,
The proudest title man can claim,
You've heard from me on land and sea
For with my name stands, VICTORY!

I ask no better lot to see,
Than that of citizen, so free,
Soldier, or sailor, let me be,
So with my name stands, LIBERTY!

Great deeds, with us, are natural things,
The power, that from within us springs,
Compels our deeds to fit the needs
Of every great emergency.

Impelled we go to face our foe,
Trusting in God, who ne'er said No!
To sacred plan, for bettering man,
And blessing all futurity.

Our patriots bold, in songs of old
Their names, are household words, oft-told,
But, "Many a name unknown to fame,
Lacked merely opportunity."

Heroes, 'tis clear, in humble sphere,
God sees and loves, as truly, here,
And up in Heaven, credit is given,
'Twill show in spotless purity.

All martyrs, brave, on ocean wave,
On sea, on shore, or in the grave,
In noble cause, their lives who gave,
Heaven is their home eternally.

Thus, with our trust in God, so just,
If "Die we may, or die we must,"
We volunteer without a fear,
For any sudden urgency.

DEWEY'S FEAT.

Of Dewey's feat with Spanish fleet,
He sunk it, needless to repeat,
All nations raise paeans of praise
And shout his name tumultuously.

Each ship and man of each proud name
That helped our Dewey humble Spain
Braved mines, torpedoes; great the gain
'Mid cannon's din uproariously.

The Petrel, small, flew like a streak,
Accomplished miracles so neat,
In which large ships could not compete,
Then made way for them gracefully.

The Olympia, Dewey's flagship, there.
In thick of fight, was everywhere.
Captain Hodgson's bravery will compare
With any in records military.

Brave Captain Gridley, since is dead,
Of hurts received there, so 'tis said,
His name cannot and will not die,
'Twas born for immortality.

As long as time and nations run,
These deeds shall shine forth as the sun,
Manila Bay, where Spain's ships lay,
They captured, hold successfully.

And there they wait in Cavite's gate
For reinforcements. Happy fate!
Our flag floats free on every sea.
Sun sets not on our territory.

Now they protect Manila town
From being pillaged up and down,
Insurgents, going to and fro,
Restrain from acts of cruelty.

Now Fifty-first Iowa boys must go
Out to help Dewey. They'll not be slow!
They, full of vim, go in to win
Their share of laurals, deservedly.

CARDENAS BAY.

The battle in Cardenas Bay,
Where, full of mines, the harbor lay,
Furnished five martyrs, no child's play!
The Winslow crippled hopelessly;

Each ship and man that in there went
To search out cables, they were bent.
Frank Newcomb, of the Hudson went
And brought her out, Oh, valiantly!

When roll was called these five were dead.
"Killed by one shell," the message said,
Ensign Worth Bagley, Raleigh, N. C.
While raising cables defiantly.

Fireman J. V. Meek and John Dunfee,
Josiah Tunnell, John Varvares,
Bravely, the world can plainly see
Doing their duty, heroically!

Bold Bernadou, hurrah for you!
William Patterson, fireman, too!
R. E. Cox, the gunner's mate,
Wounded, none seriously.

Daniel McKeon and Charles Gray,
All standing at their posts that day,
Won great renown that 12th of May,
Mid shot and shell, gloriously!

Long live each name on scrolls of fame,
Written in letters as of flame,
There every one, each gallant son
Revealed his land, Columbia!

BOTTLING OF CERVERA'S FLEET.

Schley's "bottling" of Cervera's fleet,
Is well considered something neat,
"Stopping the bottle" all repeat,
"It must go down in history!"

(Right here we note, Lieutenant Blue,
Took hardest task, himself to do,
Circled the bay, to gain a view
Of Cervera's ships, most secretly.

In utmost danger was he there,
Both night and day and some declare
That with great deeds, his will compare,
Exceeding all in difficulty.)

When call was made for volunteers,
Hundreds offered, void of fears,
They wished to go, command said, No!
Eight men can solve this mystery.

Of how to silence Spain's loud boasts,
And help to rid poor Cuba's coasts
Of tyrants chain, forged there by Spain,
In acts of treacherous cruelty.

HOBSON.

Said R. P. Hobson, here's my crew,
Daniel Montague, tried and true.
John E. Murphey, George Charette, too,
Osborn Deignan, in unity.

John Kelley, John P. Phillips, too,
Brave, willful Clausen. Now adieu
Merrill, go back! Powell, you
Watch in your launch. Now, eternity!

When asked, "what chance for life have you?"
Said Hobson, "That we can't tell true,
Thats another question," pretty blue!
But in we go for certainty.

'Twas Hobson's choice, he had full voice,
All, going with him, did rejoice,
Brave hundreds, so, did long to go,
He almost gained their enmity.

But Hobson knew just what to do,
Of men he wanted just these few,
Batteries to face, each in his place,
They did so, with impunity.

On, on they went on business bent,
So glad that they could thus be sent,
While those behind were not content
To miss the opportunity,

To outwit Spain, avenge Maine,
Give there their lives, help victory gain;
Willing to suffer death and pain
In cause of freedom, manfully:

In Santiago's Channel ran,
Held steady on, nor lost a man;
Blew up that shack, the Merrimac,
And took their chances cheerfully.

Through iron hail and leaden rain,
Not once did quail, but rowed amain,
Were taken prisoners: Not in vain!
Their act thrills all humanity.

Cervera's admiration ran
For them ran so high he sent his man
With flag of truce: That proves
God's plan: They're saved. Oh, Immortality!

Now to all men they speak again;
"We are Americans." Amen!
We're Hobson's choice, still we rejoice
Although so long in jeopardy.

"All honor to these heroes give!
Honor to all! Long may they live!
A gallant band on sea or land,
Who fight for Human Liberty.

GUAUTANAMO.

At Gautanamo our brave marines
Landed, camped there 'mid dismal scenes:
A bare hillside, no sheltering screens,
While Spanish foe skulked stealthily.

First raised our flag on Cuban soil,
Did thus the Dons defy and foil;
Held well their ground and lost no spoil,
In spite of Spanish musketry.

Four braves are killed by wily foe
Secreted in the bush below;
To bury them their comrades go
From work at trenches, silently.

The chaplain reads the service o'er
Four graves, while shot around them pour;
"Resurrection, life, forevermore,"
Through Christ, accepted it reverently.

What bolder deed can history bring,
More daring, than where bullets sing
To raise the flag? The world does ring
With praises for their bravery.

LA QUASIMA.

At the battle of La Quasima
Roosevelt and Wood here led the way;
Troops boldly climbed the hills that day,
'Mongst prickly cactus cheerfully.

Rough riders, bold, rushed on ahead
Of other troops. At first they led
On narrow path. Sixteen shot dead
And fifty wounded seriously.

First Regular Cavalry, so grand,
Proudly in every need they stand,
Rushed in, laid low the vaunting foe,
Came quick to rescue valiantly.

We've "Iowa boys" in every place—
Where danger is they're there to face;
They do their share with native grace,
And wear their laurels modestly.

To Santiago all are bent,
Its capture Shafter's firm intent;
Past barb wires, trenches, to pitch tent
At Morro Castle triumphantly.

SANTIAGO.

Saturday, the 2d of July,
This news on telegraph did fly
From Santiago, bulletined high;
Hard fighting, resisting stubbornly.

"Our men advance in bold attack,"
No Spanish horde can drive them back;
Pando's forces, alas! alack!
Reinforce the fort tremendously.

Sixty men, tried, bold and true,
From each regiment, without ado
Cut wires that others may pass through
That hell of battle, heroically.

EL CANEY HEROES.

El Caney heroes rushed ahead,
Waiting not to be sent or led,
Oh, many, many were shot dead,
And more were wounded seriously.

In thickest fight at cannon's mouth,
What is that sound comes floating forth?
"Say, can you see," both South and North
Join, sing the song, sweet melody.

Shrill, pure and clear, "dawns early light,"
"What so proudly we hail." God of might!
Wounded join in. Oh, wondrous sight!
"In twilight's gleaming" tremulously.

One valiant soldier, both arms gone
And wound in hip, did laugh, sing on,
Make light of suffering, count upon
The glory of the victory.

Sacrifice of such valor great,
Pen cannot write nor tongue relate;
Words are too weak, they but mock fate—
Heroes hoping so confidently!

Valor, heroism, courage, grand;
Hope, confidence, enthusiasm and
All virtues, glorious! sublime! command
Respect for heroes, adoringly!

If pen could write or tongue could tell
The pains endured, the taste of hell,
While Spanish poured their shot and shell,
Which our troops met unflinchingly,

'Twould make a volume reaching sky,
The dome, above, of Heaven so high,
But none would stop to ask us why
Our troops fought with tenacity.

Spain forced this war upon our land,
Sinking the Maine, all understand.
Treacherous butcher! Three hundred thousand
Own blood she murders, relentlessly!

Down, down with Spain! Her wicked reign
Will soon be o'er, nor come again;
Cuba has not besought in vain
Freemen, God's instrumentality.

Nations corrupt and tyrant's hand
Must perish, all, from off God's land;
Free Anglo Saxons all will band
Together for progress—LIBERTY!

July the fourth, oh! let it be
The day that proves poor Cuba free,
If in God's purpose it may be
The best for all humanity.

SAMPSON'S VICTORY.

"Sampson does it just like Dewey."
"Terrific fighting all day Saturday;"
"Morro Castle, Punto Gordo Battery,
"Pounded to dust by battleships' battery."

"The vessels of our Sampson's fleet
Have done some good work, quick and neat;
They've sunk another Spanish fleet!"
"Oh, Spain is doomed for certainty!"

MANZANILLO.

Hornet, Wampatuck and Hist,
Of Spanish ships, saw quick the list
To be full nine at Manzanillo—
Attack them without hesitancy.

Gunboat and sloop and one pontoon,
Purisama, Conception:
Two large transports here met their doom,
Too many to name consecutively.

Woe at Madrid! Spain must fall,
Hand-writing see upon the wall;
Vengeance for past crimes, one and all,
Her knell of doom rings dolefully.

REJOICINGS.

"Now let the American eagle scream!"
Details were lacking, but sun's beam
Did not retire 'til victory's gleam
Lit up the night with brilliancy.

To God give thanks! Jehovah, true,
Ordered this work our men should do;
In every peril led them through
And on to glorious victory.

"John Bull celebrates our glorious Fourth,"
Anglo Saxons from South to North,
East to West, throughout the earth,
Join now in grandest symphony.

A song all sing to God, our King:
Glory! Glory! Let it ring!
Glory! Glory! Let it ring!
Welcome, thrice welcome, VICTORY.

SUMMARY.

Our troops to front all wished to go,
Forty-ninth and Fiftieth to Cuba, Ho!
We'll hear from them full well we know—
Col. Dows, George Evans, becomingly.

At Chickamauga Park had we
The Fifty-second Iowa. All agree
That finer troops they ne'er did see,
Spoiling for fight impatiently.

At San Francisco have we there
The Fifty-first Iowa. All declare
That for good morals they'll compare
With any on earth, efficiently.

"To front" cried Bever's Battery, too,
With drill at Camp McKinley through;
Honor Linn County, all true blue,
Iowa's Fifth Artillery.

Burlington got up a battery, too,
As good and brave and bold and true—
Sixth Battery Boys, as they passed through
The towns, all cheered them lustily.

So we all cheer each volunteer,
Noble sacrifice God sees here!
May faith in God cast out all fear,
He is their friend unquestionably.

One writes, "My home none less I love,
But go, trust all to God above,
That Cubans may have such to love
As Iowans, in security."

Oh! God above, our thanks and love
For victories won. Peace, like a dove,
From main to shore, forevermore,
Can spread her pinions joyfully.

May, soon, humanity rise free
Throughout the earth from sea to sea;
May tyrants all be made to fall
And doomed to death, obscurity.

And God, oh God! our loved ones bring
Under the shadow of thy wing;
Protect them: gratefully we'll sing
Thy praise always, eternally.

And may they every foe withstand,
As, firmly marching hand in hand,
They work for progress, good and grand,
Temperance and frugality.

And may our Nation march right on
'Till, gracious Lord, Thy will be done;
On earth be given as in Thy Heaven,
Glory to God in loyalty.

And this our sonorous title be,
American, so bold and free.
American! Earth, sky and sea,
Resound throughout ETERNITY.

"Our Queen"

A TRIBUTE TO MISS GOULD.

Of every name on scrolls of fame,
Most loved from South to North,
Helen Gould's must lead them all
For true, intrinsic worth.

She's proved the fact, beyond cavil,
That riches are no bar
To tender, generous impulses,
Awakened by this war.

She is our queen, American,
Her throne the nation's heart;
We think of her nobility
And "Tears unbidden start."

Then hail to our queen, Helen Gould!
Take off your hat and shout,
We have a queen—Hurrah! hurrah!
Since war we've found it out.

Peace . . . .

The war was terrible but brief,
Now comes a sense of deep relief
To aching hearts which stood the strain,
Hoping, praying for peace again.

Mothers and fathers, sisters, wives
And sweethearts, too, prayed that the lives
Of their dear ones might yet be spared,
And longed for peace to be declared.

God heard their prayers, and so the dove
Of peace was sent on wings of love,
To bear the tidings to all men,
Good will! God reigns! Hail, peace again!

This peace for peoples far away,
Long crushed beneath Spain's cruel sway,
Far-reaching in effect will be,
To set those millions ever free.

Hail, God of might, Columbia's friend!
Hail, heroes, all! Thy work shall end
When all the earth, indeed, shall be
Forever and forever free.

History Repeats Itself . . . .

"History oft repeats itself."
"Like father, so like son."
These sayings, plain, are quoted oft
Since days of sixty-one;
Things happen in our nation here,
E'en at our very door,
Prove truth of each quotation clear—
Let's think and talk them o'er.

To free all men has been our boast,
And now we've proved it true,
What John Brown and his friends begun
Their sons have finished, through
Sympathy to colored folk,
Giving them chance to prove
Their gratitude for Lincoln's stroke
That gave them life and love.

OUR COLORED IMMUNES.

Our colored immunes go to front,
To Santiago's coast;
Their Captain, Amos W. Brandt,
Of him they well can boast;
He is the man of all most fit
To lead them, for their race
Owe to this family gratitude
Which time can ne'er efface.

His father, Honorable Isaac Brandt,
In slavery days of yore,
Helped with John Brown to pass right on,
From cruelties in store.
The colored people of that time
Who appealed to them for aid,
By what is called "Underground Railroad,"
To help them ne'er afraid.

Brandt's patriotism is well proved,
To Freedom's cause he's given
A sacrifice of business great.
The record's kept in heaven,
Credit to each and every man
Who serves his country well,
Gives up his private interests,
Our army grand to swell.

To do each duty as it comes,
To wait or go ahead;
Keep pure his record, do his best,
Be leader or be led;
Whate'er his station, be content
To do all with his might;
He is a soldier, brave and true,
Who dares to do the right.

Now grandly proud, you colored boys
Can hold your heads upright;
Although it seems there'll be no need
In battles now to fight,
You've shown your willingness to do
Your part. You've done your best,
And it is known and credit given
To you, with all the rest.

Now, McAfee and Wilburn, too,
Watch well your colored boys.
Help them to keep their good name up,
At home, 'twill cause more joys,
Than all else could, to see your name
Spoken of here with pride;
Iowa's brave immunes, you are
So known, both far and wide.

Our Fifty-second Iowa Boys.

Tune—"My Maryland."

We welcome now our soldiers home,
Iowa boys, Oh, Iowa boys!
Thank God! they're not compelled to roam.
Iowa boys, Oh, Iowa boys!

Chorus—

When war broke out they sprang to arms,
And offered life with all its charms;
Peace now has come; no more alarms;
Welcome boys! Yes, welcome, boys!

They drilled at Chickamauga Park,
Iowa boys, yes, Iowa boys!
All summer long, from dawn till dark;
Iowa boys, brave Iowa boys!

Chorus—

At grand review beyond compare,
Of forty thousand soldiers there,
"The palm the Fifty-second bear,"
"Camp Thomas News" of Iowa boys.

"As straight as arrows were each line,"
Iowa boys, of Iowa boys.
"With faultless step and clock-work time,"
Iowa boys, all Iowa boys.

Chorus—

"The men were of splendid physique,"
Their execution nothing weak,
In plaudits multitudes did speak
Of Fifty-second Iowa boys.

And now they're home, All hail! All hail!
Fifty-second Iowa boys!
Each duty done, in naught did fall,
Our Fifty-second Iowa boys.

Chorus—

Those lost to earth have gone before
To Jordan's ever peaceful shore;
Angels bore them safely o'er;
Iowa boys, God's Iowa boys.

When decoration day comes round,
Iowa girls, Oh, Iowa girls!
With choicest roses strew each mound,
Iowa girls, Oh, Iowa girls!

Chorus—

Keep ever green their memories, too,
They gave their all, these boys in blue,
What more could mortal heroes do
For God and home and Iowa girls?

Ghosts! . . . .

Yes, there was a ghost in the house,
There must have been;
Keep still as a mouse
While I tell you.

Just mother and baby and I
Lived in the big house all alone:
It is full good two stories high,
The foundation is made of stone.
There are nine large rooms in the house,
And closets and garrets beside—
Just plenty and plenty of room
Where a real live ghost could hide.

It's kind of run down as they say
So some one just pulled off a board
On the north side, to see if the sills
Were rotten or with worm eating scored,
And the cellar needs fixing a bit,
Though the wall is thick and strong,
The outside cellarway is filled up,
Not been used for ever so long.

It's a lonesome place at the best,
For it stands far back from the road,
And the weeds, round, had grown pretty high,
For they had not lately been mowed,
And the trees had many dead limbs
That reached out so stark, gray and bare,
When we came home from church at night,
Seemed they'd clutch us by the hair.

The ideal place for a ghost
But we were not one bit afraid.
But, "What's that?" mother asks, "Hear that?"
And, thump, thump, up stairs, the noise made.
"It sounds like some one with a cane;"
And a story we'd often heard
Flashed over our minds at once,
And I tell you we hardly stirred.

A real old, lame man once lived here.
All alone, by himself, it's said;
He'd money 'twas thought, but none knew,
And one morning he was found, dead,
Up stairs in one of the bed rooms
With a paper clutched in his hand:
'Twas written quite plain, "There's my cash,
I'll come back for it, understand?"

But nobody understood it,
And the money no one could find,
Though they searched in every cranny.
So at length, it passed out of mind.
But, "Hear that? There it goes! Thump, thump!"
It's just like the noise of his cane,
Superstitious we will not be
But, there it goes, "Thump, thump" again.

"Are you brave? A light! Let's go up!
We'll see what's going on up stairs."
"Here's the broom, there's the rolling pin,
No one shall take us unawares,"
"Hold the light, high," rooms all empty,
Not a sound! "Yes, there is a sigh!"
A presence there, invisible,
We thought, to the poor naked eye.

"If it is his spirit, restless,
Come back to his money or wealth,
"Would he hurt us?" "By no means,
So watch, we'll find out, not by stealth,"
For at nine each night we heard him,
And, so, up the stairway we went,
Light in hand; "Kind ghost what ails you?
Are you restless, not now content?"

"You can tell us where's your money,
We'd make use of it right, you'd see,
We'd give to the poor and needy,
And a hospital we would fee:
How glad we'd be to be able .
To do all the good we've heard,
And have the news go on the cable
As swift as the flight of a bird!"

"We'd fit out a hospital ship
If money to us came by chance,
We'd do like Miss Barton or Gould
Whose great names their good deeds enhance;
Or good Mrs. Leiter who gave
Hospital at Chickamauga Park,
For soldiers work, early and late,
From day's dawn 'till long after dark."

"Large boxes of good things we'd send
To all of our boys in blue,
Or buff, or gray, or whatever
The uniform, so they are true
To God and their country and home,
Though ever so far, far away,
We'd care for their families too,
During all their long, tedious stay."

"Mr. Ghost, now, why won't you tell
Where the money is, right away?
We really are tired of planning
For things, for which we can't pay."
But he never answered a word,
Although he came back every night,
And, "Thump, thump, thump, thump," went
    his cane
From nine o'clock 'til morning light.

Some folks said, "Oh, I'd be so scared
On hearing that ghost every night!"
Well, we were, somewhat, at the first,
But at last it seemed to be right;
For we wished and hoped he'd tell us
His secret and give us the cash;
At length, well, fact, we beheld him!
And, our grand hopes, all, went to smash.

It came 'round about, in this wise
One day when we'd all been away,
We came back to the house next ours
And sat down, a short time to stay,
We noticed the dogs were racing,
And sniffing and smelling around
And wagging their tails while running
With noses close down to the ground.

All at once to our house chasing
To the north side with a long bound,
Where the board was off the siding,
And, "What is it they're dragging 'round?"
A full grown hare, Mr. Rabbit,
Who'd tried to get inside in vain,
Still, we looked for our ghost that night,
But he never came back again.

The mystery, I will tell you
How he could "Thump, thump, thump," up stairs
The corner gnawed off a loft door
In the hallway there, unawares
To us, had been his ingress
From over the kitchen room:
His egress too, when up we came
With rolling pin, light and broom.

We lost confidence then in ghosts,
Even ghosts of happier days,
Saw, we our own duties must do,
Covet wealth not, nor sweet words of praise:
The work that seemed nearest we did,
Though, truly, we longed, much, for more
And now we are wondering how
Opportunities closed, locked door
Shall be ope'd that we may do more.

For we picked blackberries bravely,
Though they scratched our poor hands full **sore**,
Then made them into jams and jell,
And earnestly wished there were more:
Small gift, we're going to send it
To the hospital store it'll add:
For boys in blue, or buff, or gray,
If ten times as much we'd be glad:
There's so little it makes us feel sad.

But we picked and gleaned and got scratched,
We searched the patch over again.
Two score of jell glasses we filled,
Then stopped. The berries were gone.
I think, now, I'll go and take them
And visit the hospital corps
And offer myself as a nurse;
Mayhap opportunity's door
Might ope if they need just one more.

Welcome Home, Fiftieth Iowa.

Tune—"BEULAH LAND," repeat last two lines in every second verse.

The Fiftieth Iowa boys are home,
And oh, how glad we are they've come!
And glad were they to see the dome
Of Iowa's State Capitol.

This regiment, the first to go
To Jacksonville, 'twas southward, Ho!
Then war was meant, full well we know,
And knew 'twas unavoidable.

They went without a murmur, too,
These bonny boys, "Our boys in blue,"
We're proud of them, each patriot true,
Their conduct was commendable.

All summer long they waited there
Hoping of fight to get their share,
But now, the nations peace declare,
Desire for home is laudable.

They met and did each duty well,
And thus will page of history tell.
Take off your hats! Shout! Let us swell
A welcome to them audible.

When Fiftieth Iowa came away,
General Lee was heard to say
He much had hoped they were to stay
With him, these boys most honorable.

He'd rather lose any regiment
That to him thus far had been sent;
From Seventh Corps when Fiftieth went,
His loss was irreparable.

Col. Lambert, too, their friend so true,
Stands by these boys, his boys in blue;
He holds their good traits all in view
Their love for him is remarkable.

Of those who went not all are here,
To soldier boys Heaven must be near;
For life they've given without a fear,
Oh, sacrifice most wonderful!

Those gone before, say not they're dead,
They've life immortal, God has said,
With crown, too, placed upon each head
Of martyr: Boon unspeakable!

We know God sees the sparrows fall,
Will He not much more save them, all
These heroes, who obeyed the call
Of country, now made memorable?

Cedar Rapids . . .

Cedar Rapids the pride of Linn County,
Of Eastern Iowa, the gem,
To the soldiers, her hospitality
Is known, and approved, of all men.

Her light can't be hid neath a bushel,
But must shine and be seen from afar,
Attracting and drawing attention
Like the beams of a glorious star.

With banquets, soft pillows and cushions,
Hopeful poems, prayers and good cheer,
The kind comfort committee-men met them
And gave them a home welcome here.

Thankful letters received from Rough Riders,
All soldiers who've passed through this way,
Say your kindness will ne'er be forgotten,
High your aim, proud your name, good deeds stay.

And the bread that is cast upon water
After days will come back, 'tis said,
In great bounty, return to the giver
With blessings, too, showered on his head.

Song—Helen Gould

Tune—"Sweet Marie."

I've a tale I'd tell to you, Helen Gould,
But the half of it can never be told,
For here's all these boys in blue
And their friends who love them true,
Offering thanks and love to you, Helen Gould.

I am speaking for them all, Helen Gould,
And I hope that you will not deem me bold,
When I say of hearts you're queen,
Best, most generous ever seen,
And all love you best, I ween, Helen Gould.

When this Spanish war broke out, Helen Gould,
And the soldiers to the front went, so bold,
Then this queen to front came too,
Showed her patriotism true
By her aid to boys in blue, Helen Gould.

You have shown yourself a queen, Helen Gould,
And a crown you're lacking not, 'twill be told
In all history 'twill be found,
Everlastingly you're crowned,
Nation's cheers will ne'er be drowned, Helen Gould.

The Naval Parade . . .

At New York, August 20, 1898.

'Tis a day, yes, to be long, long remembered,
New York's citizens all did their best
To give rousing enthusiastic welcome
To the fleet and to Sampson, their guest.

The celebration was grand, all impromptu,
But the flagship New York had scarce there
Entered Narrows till shores of Staten Island
Were lined, standing room, none to spare.

Also Long Island shores and New Jersey
Were black with great multitudes in wait,
And 'long the docks of New York city
Gathered citizens, it seemed the whole state.

From the windows of all the tall buildings,
And up along Riverside Drive,
Naught but countless masses of people,
For conquerors their cheers, all alive!

Grim battle ships showed but small sign of fight
With Cervera's long boasted great fleet;
The damage, if any, must have been very light,
Received there in sinking them neat.

First came flagship New York from mainmast
 of which
Admiral Sampson's twin star flag of blue
Was flying, and which was then in command
Of Captain F. E. Chadwick, so true.

Next came the Iowa, Captain Evans in command,
Indiana, Captain Taylor, and tars,
Then Brooklyn sailed proudly, while bearing along
Admiral Schley's blue flag with two stars.

She was under command of brave Captain Cook,
Followed by Massachusetts in wake,
Her commander's name, Captain Higginson:
Many pages of history 'twill take

To record half the prowess of next one in line,
Famous Oregon, whose wonderful speed
Was shown in chasing Christobal Colon
In the hour when it stood in good need.

The outspoken admiration of the whole world
Had been given to her, when before
She had sailed neath her banner, so bright, unfurled,
From Pacific to Atlantic shore.

She was followed by one, once known as Hoodoo,
Now, the Texas, which has brushed from her side
Her former cognomen, and now she is known
As a fighting machine, far and wide.

The Massachusetts was dirty, 'twas said:
"Respectably dirty" said one
Heavy duty makes dirt, we'll not be illbred
And find fault when that duty's well done.

The vessels proceeded then up the Hudson
As far as our General Grant's tomb,
Fired salutes, turned around, went down the river,
At Governor's Island stopped a short time.

Then proceeded to anchorage off Tompkinsville,
And now long remembered 'twill be,
By New Yorkers and others who saw the parade
As something most glorious to see.

'Twas an impressive spectacle there to behold,
For these vessels, their guns and their crews,
Had been history making all summer so bold,
To no one is this any news.

They had won for their country new glories, fame,
Those who nobly had stood behind guns
Could be seen standing there on the forward deck came
Bold heroes, the very same ones.

Responding most heartily to cheers of the crowd,
Enjoying this rest from their toil;
Reward for their labors, this calling aloud
Of praise ne'er our heroes can spoil.

Not much time did they have to prepare for parade,
But what the New Yorkers could do
To honor these ships and their men was there done,
In remembrance this day'll be held, too.

As long as generations shall hand records down
Of heroic deeds: bold, fearless, brave,
These heroes with laurels and victory's crown
Shall live beyond confines of grave.

Yes, forever shall live on history's page,
As glorious those deeds, there, sublime,
As are told of bold warriors of any age,
Any country or any fair clime.

Re=United . . .

Re-united! Re-united!
Write the word across the sky.
Let all nations read the story,
Hold aloft our banner high:
Glorious banner! born of freedom!
And where'er its proud folds wave
There shall tyranny, oppression,
Loose their bonds, release each slave!

Men and brothers, one time foemen,
Now are comrades, each one true
To one banner, Union Banner,
Stars and Stripes, "Red, White and Blue."
Let old scores be now forgotten,
Union's bands more closely tie,
North and South *are one forever*,
Foes beware, and come not nigh!

War is dreadful: well we know it,
And the civil war, long past,
We had hoped and fully counted
That it long would be the last:
But the cries of thousands murdered
At our very threshold, door,
Pierced our hearts, we sent them succor,
Spain is humbled, war is o'er.

Now let peace and plenty calm us,
Let no niggard hand supply,
Cut down navies or defences,
Of our nation make a guy;
As in years of reconstruction,
Parsimonious plans combined
Had of us almost constructed
Laughing stock for all mankind:

When at length war did confront us
In all haste we did prepare,
Some mistakes occurred to teach us
Consequence of niggard's care
In preventing appropriations
For defense in time of peace,
Thinking that our size and prowess
Should compel all war to cease.

Now the same ones who prevented
Us from having safe supplies
Are, with ready adaptation,
Filling all the world with cries
In regard to gross abuses,
And neglect they now complain,
Can't they see their parsimony
Helped to cause this war with Spain?

Caused contempt and gross defiance
For appearance of our fleet,
When at length the Maine was blown up
Then raged vengeance at white heat:
Bills were passed, appropriations,
Half of which had done more good
As preventives, during peace times,
Than all rush and hurry could.

But our President, McKinley,
With firm, wise and honest hand,
Held back hasty demonstrations,
Took a bold and steadfast stand;
And in spite of much traducing
Rose above all, towering high,
Gave his orders, set in motion
Wheels of factories for supply.

Miracles were then accomplished
In the few short days to spare.
While proceed investigations
On the "Maine" and treachery there:
Then "To arms!" our boys are rushing,
North and South and East and West;
Each one vieing with the other
To show their love of land the best.

Then came splendid feats of valor,
Grand achievements, deeds sublime,
Waking general admiration
From all lands in every clime.
Then majestic swept our navy,
Scoured the seas in search of foes,
And with aid of Shafter's army
Brought the war to speedy close.

Long the list of names of heroes,
Well they're known, no need to tell;
But of all they did most glorious,
Praise ring long and loud and well:
All who offered, gave their service
To their country in her need,
Every private, each one honor;
Give to each of praise his meed.

To the front all wished to hasten.
Forward rush, with hasty speed,
But the shortness of the conflict
That forbade, there was no need;
Those left out were disappointed,
Glories fell not to their share;
Thus they thought and still keep thinking
But they're wrong we must declare.

For our President, McKinley.
Says, to each one falls his share,
All were willing, all were anxious
To go forward, do and dare.
'Twas no fault of our brave army
That all fighting could not see,
Or rush forward. "On to Cuba!"
Help to set poor Cubans free.

For when war so soon was over
Fighting would not reach around
To give soldiers, every regiment,
Chance to carry home a wound;
But we honor their intention,
And their wish to front to go
Just as much deserve our plaudits,
Bravery, courage, all did show.

Those in camps who watched and waited
For their summons to the front,
Were as ready, yes, impatient,
In this war to bear the brunt
As the soldiers who went forward,
And were just as bold and brave,
Sacrificed their good positions,
Life and all, they freely gave.

Instance Second Lieutenant Guy Kellogg,
Vinton, Iowa's honored son;
Manly, upright, most industrious,
Who to front his way had won
For himself a place of standing,
In esteem most highly held,
Interested in military discipline,
In its tactics thoroughly drilled.

Advanced by free choice of his comrades
In the guards until the call
Came, in Co. G, Forty-ninth Iowa,
Guy Kellogg then gives all:
Wife so cherished, all bright prospects,
Law's successes, bright career,
Went forth then a Forty-ninth soldier,
Proud with others, void of fear.

Spent a few days home in Vinton,
After the regiment had gone south,
Chief of the recruiting detail,
In the audience on the Sabbath,
During patriotic services
On the 3d day of July,
Chaplain Mason's letter called for
Tent, he spoke and told us why.

What good work and great advantage
The proposed tent would be to all,
Forty-ninth Iowa boys in particular.
And the tent was sent at call.
In obedience then to orders,
To his duties was assigned,
This our youth, acting Judge Advocate
Of the brigade to which he belonged.

Next came sorrow to his dear ones,
Brave young wife, so soon bereft,
Brought the lifeless body with her
Of her hero, all that's left.
Does it seem that all this treasure
Has been wasted, useless been?
No; there is God keeps record,
Counts each sacrifice and gives crown.

This is one alone of many
We could cite did space permit;
Noble, talented, most gifted,
And for highest calling fit;
Gave up lucrative positions,
Went to front at duty's call;
But these pages could not hold them
Did we try to name them all.

Each proud name give highest honor,
Soldier brave and bold was he;
Matters not he saw not battle,
Hardships saw he, all agree:
And each soldier is entitled
To our thanks for duties done;
All endured for sake of country,
Most glorious beneath the sun.

Captain Goodrell . . .

Mancel Goodrell, who, at Guantanamo,
Raised our flag on Cuban soil,
Is a modest Iowa hero
Whom no flattery e'er can spoil:

In two wars he stands before us,
For since times of sixty-one
He's been in the regular army;
Proud we claim him Iowa's son:

He was in the Fifteenth Regiment,
Co. B, of Volunteers,
Crocker's Iowa Brigade soldiers,
All are heroes void of fears.

Deeds of valor all accomplished
During days of bloody war,
Now these comrades glad would greet him,
Those from near and those from far.

W. A. Boudinot, one among them,
Enlisted when not quite fifteen,
Taken prisoner at Atlanta,
At Andersonville he soon was seen.

After six months' life in prison
He and others gained parole,
But the weakened, broken body
Scarcely could contain each soul.

All through life was weakness master,
Never gained he normal strength,
So was tied, in effort hindered,
'Till God called, him home at length,

To the land where all the humble
Heroes, there, are glorified,
All is known there, how each noble
Soldier, offered life and died.

Thus their ranks are thinned and broken,
Death has claimed of heroes, brave,
Greater share; the word was spoken;
Silent lie they in the grave.

But their deeds are ne'er forgotten,
In immortal light shall shine,
Long as patriots and sages
Bow at freedom's holy shrine.

Their example set before us
Fires our youth with strong desire
Front to go and there do likewise,
To emulate them all aspire.

"Goodbye comrades," God be with you,
May all meet above in heaven,
There the humblest one among you
Can be sure of credit given.

BIRDIE V. BOUDINOT.

THE SOLDIER'S DAUGHTER

Peace Jubilee . . .

October 18, 1898.

Formal opening of the Peace Jubilee
In progress at Chicago to-day,
Auditorium packed in the morning to hear
What McKinley and others will say.

Six vials of eloquence there were outpoured,
Making launching a decided success,
With patriotism, prudence and wisdom well
    stored
Was each utterance and able address.

Rev. Frank W. Gunsaulus offered the prayer,
Chairman Truax made opening address,
Introduced George R. Peck presiding officer,
Who respects paid the city's great guest.

Mr. Peck said: "One name in this pageantry
    here,
In your thoughts and your hearts will speak
    out,
The name of our President McKinley most
    dear,
You know him and what he's about.

Wise, patient, kindly, most generous and calm,
And judging of that which is right
And highest in statesmanship, takes there the
    palm,
How surely he knows upon sight,

How surely he knows, as here now he must,
When his countrymen he meets face to face,
Always the people their leader will trust
Who trusts to good conscience and grace.

We cannot say, yet, that all dangers are passed,
Some storms may come, some waves roll high,
But know a brave, strong hand guides rud-
    der, stays mast,
Sights breakers ahead with keen eye."

Mr. Peck introduced then Archbishop Ireland,
Who the closest attention received,
Being frequently compelled to remain silent
'Till outbursts of applause were relieved.

His address was in part as follows, now, here:
War has passed, peace reigns, is supreme,
Stilled o'er land and o'er sea is the shrill
    clang of arms,
Our banner floats in the sun's gleam.

From San Juan heights to far Manila
Floats fearless, triumphant and bold,
The Star Spangled Banner, Oh! America,
Be glad and rejoice heart and soul.

Celebrate, Oh! peace, now, thy grand jubilee,
Heaven's gift are thou ever to earth,
When Savior of humanity in Bethlehem was born,
The stars and the sky then sang forth.

"Glory to God in the highest!" on high,
On earth, peace and good will to men,
Peace through Christ, our Lord, ever nigh,
Peace when spirit of Christ is supreme.

Oh! peace, so precious to humanity.
Art thou, that our highest ideal
Of social felicity ever must be
On earth, thy sovereignty, real.

Pagan statesmanship through poetry exclaims;
"Best of things which 'tis given men to know
Is peace," better far than a thousand triumphs,
Simple gift of peace, there to show.

The regenerated world shall not lift up the sword,
Against sword, neither then shall they know
Or be exercised any more, then, in war,
For peace is the normal outflow

Of humanity's life, the healthy pulse beat;
Of social organism, growth;
The vital condition of happiness complete,
How lovely, delightful, thou'rt both!

Praise of peace is proclaimed beyond all need
    of words,
When all men are prone to confess
That the only possible justification of war
Is establishment, firmly, of peace.

War, how dreadful thou art! but I shall not
    declare
Thee unnecessary, immoral, accursed,
Mete out condemnation to history past
Of my America and nations of earth.

But, that thou art dreadful, ever barbarous
I shall not e'en attempt to deny.
War, is it design, cunning, in order to hide
Thy true nature from manhood's clear eye

That circumstance, pomp, attend ever thy
    march,
That poetry and music supply
Through thy heavy darkness, the struggling
    rays, bright,
History weaves into glories so high?

Stripped bare of thy show and tinsel so gay;
What art thou but slaying of men
By thousands, aye, often ten thousands we say,
And hundreds of thousands again?

With most steady aim and relentless energy
Taxing science to ingenuity utmost,
Multitudes of men to endurance by day
And by night, throughout all their coasts ;

To make preparation for war in all haste
Taxes utmost the power of might,
Armies meet on the field to kill and to waste
Like leaves, in autumnal storms' flight.

Men fall to ground bleeding, dying, the earth
Is reddened by best human blood,
The more gory the path the louder sounds
    forth
Cheers of victors who wade through death's
    flood.

This, this is the actual conflict of war.
From North to South and East to West,
Throughout both countries, whose flags were
    raised o'er
Field of battle where struggle their best;

Is soul-wrecking grief for husband, father,
Son or brother who sank neath the steel
Of foeman, on battle ground dying there,
Or the death that vile fevers oft deal,

Or, sorrowing, he comes an invalid home,
A maimed, weakened body has he,
Yet they're thankful he's spared and e'en thus can come,
This, result of war is; all can see.

Reduced to the smallest sacrifice of life,
The carnage of the battle field,
There's some one has died and some one's bereft,
E'en if headline reads "Only one killed."

"Only one," cries the newsboy, "Only one killed,"
Cries the mother, "Oh, he was my son!
What were a thousand, a regiment filled
To this one, my hero, my own;"

It was Wellington who said, "Take my word for it,
If you'd seen but one day of war
You would pray to your God that never you might
Such a thing see again," e'en afar.

'Twas Napoleon who said, "The sight of battle field,
After fight, is enough to inspire
Princes and kings with a strong love of peace
And a horror of warfare," so dire,

War, be thou gone from my soul's inner sight,
I thank the good God, now, that war
Ghastly spectre 's no longer on threshold of home
Or threatens in distant lands, far.

I ask high heaven, "Shall humanity rise
To such heights of reason that war
Shall be impossible and stories of fights
Be but echoes to sadden and mar."

And yet, while we wait that far blessed day
When embodied justice shall stand
In judgment, 'tween peoples as 'tween individuals;
Conditions, repellant, demand

Removal of causes which stand in the way,
Of dictates of reason and right,
Failing in all other inducements may
Impose war, to decide it by might.

We love peace, not war, but when to war
    we go
We send of our bravest and best,
Of the country; our magistrate, chief, says so,
Great principles embody and test.

America's too great to be shut from the
    world,
She's a world power whose voice echoes far,
Whose quick spirit travels 'cross mountains
    and seas
And lights up the world like a star.

And with America goes far and wide
What, in grandest ideal, she displays;
Democracy, liberty, good government
By the people, for the people, we praise.

If ever 'twas allowed o'er result of their wars
To nations their voices to raise;
America, to-day, should now lift up her voice
In this jubilee, now, chant her praise,

Not of war, but of peace, let praises rebound;
Her greatness, imperative it makes,
That praises of peace though the whole land
    resound;
Praise of peace, now, for all nations' sakes.

America, the eyes of the world are on thee;
Thou livest for all the whole world,
The new era's shedding its light, plain to see,
Out through thee upon the whole world.

I am dazed by thy power, responsibility to God,
Am affrighted thy greatness to see;
Thou failing, democracy, liberty fail;
In the earth is no land of the free.

Americans, your country demands virtue clear,
Intelligence bright as the day,
Build school houses, colleges, drive from the land
Ignorance and darkness away.

Let America be of honesty the home,
Justice, purity, obedience to law,
Temperance, faithfulness and honor come,
Virtue leads, in this march, without flaw.

And now, America, land of our pride,
Our love and our hope, we now place
Thee, to-day and to-morrow, in hands of our guide,
The almighty God, Lord of all space.

Chairman Peck introduced Judge Speer, of
    Georgia,
Who against him had fought long ago,
As one of the fighting rebels, then led
By Wheeler, "Our brave Fighting Joe."

Judge Speer delivered a scholarly address,
Spanish history going into at length,
Showing traditions, character, inimical
To American freedom and strength.

Closing as follows: May the wasted and worn
Followers of Gomez and Garcia
Come to appreciate the blessings of liberty
    won:
Wish and aim of Americans to-day.

We would not be their masters e'en if we
    could,
Our gigantic power was put forth,
Their salvation, pacification accomplish we
    would,
So we pledge them, before the whole earth.

We will labor with them, secure justice and
    peace
And the blessings of liberty's sway,
Domestic tranquility, general welfare
  To themselves and their posterity.

For the common defence in blue ether, above
The beautiful isle of Cuba,
Is poised our grand eagle in proud watchful
    love
To protect her, forever and aye.

An unspeakable blessing to all of mankind
In the struggle from which we've emerged,
Is the genuine, brotherly sympathy shown
By the English; strong friendship is urged.

As Olympia, Dewey's flagship steamed slowly
    into line
Of battle, at Manilla there,
As she passed British flagship, the Immortalite,
Its band rang out the inspiring air.

"See the conquering hero," now here he comes;
As Olympia flung ensign to air,
Came from our kinsman, o'er waters again,
Thrilling "Star Spangled Banner," so fair.

Then duty was on us in sight of God and
    mankind
The unholy policy to stay,
(Which, as demonstrated before senate com-
    mittee,
Had, in one year, resulted this way;

Starvation for two hundred thousand men,
Women and children, this slow
And torturing death, life denied, when to them
In a half a day's sail we could go,)

To this purpose our President devoted all art
Of his resourceful nature, sublime,
Moderate, considerate plans of his great heart,
Christian magnanimity, in vain.

Finally when investigation had developed the
 truth,
How our gallant seamen were slain
Remorselessly, cruelly, treacherous and ruth,
By the Spanish in sinking the Maine,

We had been despicable on historic page,
To "God of Battles," not have appealed,
Seventy million of people cried aloud in their
 rage,
Then, the fate of the murderers was sealed.

Our navy so noble, swift sped to its task,
Let the waters that moan through the wrecks,
Fire distorted hulls, answer question you ask,
How to Spain our navy paid debts.

Nor is the renown to our army one whit
Less glorious; nothing in lucid page
Of Thucydides, nor in Caesar's comment
Can our thoughts e'er more nobly engage.

Can this story of how, be ever surpassed,
Spurning chapparal and the barb wire,
Pressing rifles close, closer to each throbbing
    breast,
Up heights they toiled on, facing fire,

The machine guns and mausers mowing their
    best,
As if with a reaper of might,
On, on, yes right on, 'till they won fiery crest
And victory, yes victory, in sight.

With Israel's royal poet exclaim;
"Sing unto the Lord a new song,
For marvelous things hath he done," bless His
    name,
In His hand doth He hold victory, strong,

America, humane, in triumph's sweet hour,
To vanquished most gentle and kind:
To thee, Lord God of hosts, for thus giving
    us power,
Most grateful are we, of one mind.

In unity, grand, we before the world stand
And none dispute with us our sway,
As the sands of the sea, so freemen shall be,
Growth as swift as the morn when 'tis day.

As soon as Judge Speer had finished loud cries
Of "McKinley! McKinley!" were heard,
The president had turned preparing to leave,
Calls continuing, he spoke in these words:

"My fellow citizens, I've been deeply moved,
Deeply touched by the words which you say,
Patriotism uttered by distinguished men
In your presence, eloquently, to-day.

It is gratifying, now, to us all
To know, that this war did not cease
To be, a war at humanity's call,
A war in the interests of peace.

The last ship that went out of Havana harbor
Before the war was declared,
Was an American ship, that had taken supplies
To Cuba, there to be shared.

And the first ship to sail into Santiago harbor
Was an American ship bearing food,
Supplies, to the suffering inhabitants there,
To do them all possible good.

And I'm sure universal American prayers
That justice, civilization reign,
And the final settlement of peace characterize
As they've distinguished war's progress, plain.

My countrymen, the current of destiny flows
Through the hearts of the people, who will
Check them, divert them, stop them, God knows
Moves of destiny: He planned they'll fulfill."

As the President retired there were, for Oglesby, calls,
Who made a few remarks, closing them
With a call for "Three cheers for McKinley" all,
Which were given with a rousing good will.

The forenoon's exercises ended with song
"America," a rendition by band;
Enthusiasm carried the people along,
So, upward they rise, there they stand.

During the afternoon in various parts
Of the city, were held meetings, where
One was addressed by Gen. Miles, Gen. H. M. Duffield
And Booker Washington in Columbia Theater.

Gen. Miles it was, made the principal address,
It being this, in part, as follows:
Our government carried us through vicissitudes
To a violent and destructive war's close;

Has given us an unbroken chapter of victories
In wars with foreign countries, all four.
We may have thought lightly of our relations
With other governments of yore,

Or of army, navy, which, to represent
Physical force of our nation do stand,
Yet now we have in this late Spanish war
Witnessed proudly an uprising, grand!

The very flower of our splendid manhood,
The noble, patriotic and brave,
Crowding avenues, as those going to festival
    would,
Seeking front ranks, war's paths to the grave.

Privation and suffering, they counted not cost,
North and South vied each with other to show
Their devotion to country, all in unity lost
Their disruption, of long years ago.

'Tis a glorious fact, patriots were not confined
To any one section or race,
In bravery, sacrifice, all of one mind,
No regard paid to color of face.

The whites were accompanied by gallant blacks
As they swept over strong, intrenched lines;
The latter volunteered to succor the sick,
Nurse the dying, bury dead, at all times.

The navy and army of the United States
Have written, on history's page,
A chapter that's gilded with glory, and which
Every American's pride should engage.

These remarks of the commanding general
Of the army, met with favor, great,
He was again and again compelled to bow
Acknowledgments, when applause did him greet.

General Duffield, who was also greeted with
    applause,
Spoke next, advocating increase
In standing army, to meet requirements
Needed, now, even in times of peace.

Booker T. Washington was speaker next,
And his patriotic speech did evoke
Much enthusiasm, when he took for his text,
"A Much Mixed Nation," all giving heed while
    he spoke.

He said, in part, with the close of this war,
We are likely to find such a mix
Of races and tongues that the white man, I fear,
Can't identify himself, in this fix.

In fact, I feel rather anxious about
The white man, in this respect,
But not so for the negro, for there is no doubt,
His lineage all can detect.

You see, the instant it is proven, that
An individual has one per cent
Of African blood, he falls to us, flat,
He's a Negro, then, to all intent:

The 99 per cent of Anglo-Saxon blood
Counts for nothing, we claim the man
For our race, and it is well understood:
Now take him away if you can.

It's a great satisfaction, just now, to belong
To a race, when Americans, white,
Are likely to find themselves intermingled with
The Mongolians and Malays now in sight.

I say, under such circumstances, it is
A supreme satisfaction to belong
To a race, that, potential drawing powers has
Such as mine, so remarkably strong.

If there's one class of citizens has cause to rejoice,
More than another, on the outcome of this war,
'Tis the American negro, who should lift up his voice
In rejoicings, both near and afar:

'Twas known he could work, build railroads,
　　clear fields,
Raise of rice, sugar cane, cotton, more
Than the whole world could use, think of the
　　yields
Of all products, so vast, in full store:

But 'twas doubted whether or not, he could
Be depended upon, in time of need;
Liberty, honor to defend as man should,
Or was worthy of praise, a full meed.

Did he disappoint you, using bullet or sword?
As we measured up to highest test
Of manhood, at each point, where we were
　　trusted,
So believe me, each, will e'er do his best,

In the same degree, can be relied upon
To preserve and interests defend
Of this country, ever and anon;
On the colored race you can depend.

And you have it from the lips of brave Shafter,
During the six months we've been tested by
　　fire,
Roosevelt, Wheeler, Northern and Southern
　　soldier,
That we did not fail, but rose higher.

Now the tables we'll turn and on trial put you;
Preparing in property and thrift,
Economy, education and character, too,
For the duties of highest citizenship:

When we have prepared ourselves, as a race,
We shall ask you, that in every part
You accord us the same, all opportunities
That to foreigners you extend from the start,

We are going to ask, that, as color line you forgot
When that intrepid black regiment
Saved the Rough Riders, there on the spot,
You forget it in civil government,

As effectiveness of the bullet was not judged by the skin
Of the man who stood benind the gun,
That you cease to judge the value of citizenship
By curl of hair or tincture of the skin.

My friends, as we celebrate peace, let us learn
That God has been teaching old Spain
A terrible lesson; you ask what it is?
I will tell you and gratitude gain.

Simply this: that no nation can disregard
The interests of any one part
Of its members, without that nation grows weak
And corrupt and vile at its heart.

Though the penalty may have been long delayed,
God has been now teaching Spain,
That for each one of her subjects a price, must be paid
For ignorance, poverty, crimes which remain,

Could be only paid by heart of her land
And bluest blood of her sons,
With treasure beyond computation and
The loss of her fleet and her guns.

From this spectacle I pray to my God,
That a lesson, America will learn,
In respect to eight million negroes in the South,
Let her plans to educate them now turn.

There've been placed in your midst nearly ten million souls,
Who in most elements of civilization are weak,
Providence placed them here, not without a purpose,
To uplift them should you nobly seek.

One object, in my opinion, is that the stronger race,
A lesson of patience may imbibe,
Forbearance and childlike, yet supreme, trust in God
Of the universe, whate'er may betide.

This race has been placed here that the white
　　man might have
An opportunity, Ah! so great,
Of uplifting himself by uplifting us
By his interest in this race's fate.

Amidst the excitement, glamour, interest,
The deeds of heroism, that have clung
Around this, our war, let us not, now, forget
A condition that must be o'ercome:

In the southern part of our country, grand!
Deepest thoughts, generous help, most sublime,
Are needed for years, in humanity's cause
To blot ignorance, poverty, and crime,

That ne'er edict of war nor protocol of peace,
Can erase, from fair history's page,
The dread situation, should all effort cease,
Education ne'er thought more engage.

There has been, most properly, deep interest
　　shown
In the thousands of young men who've gone
From all parts of our country, in brave defense
Of our honor and humanity, well known;

But I beg you to remember, that, from our schools
And colleges, in the far south,
There are going forth, each year, thousands of young men
And women, who are teachers of worth,

Into dark, secluded corners and lonely school house,
'Midst poverty and ignorance, drear;
They're fighting battles, against common foes,
Though no drum beats, banners fly, or friends cheer;

Just as truly and bravely, as those who go forth
To do battle against foreign foe.
Now, the close of the Spanish-American war
Brings new problems, we shall meet them, we'll show:

One supreme element of danger there is:
The further as a nation we go
In the direction of engrafting into our system
Of government, the ignorant and low,

Irresponsible inhabitant of foreign lands,
The more we are tempted to depart
From those principles which have made us, as a nation, great;
Too great, for any standard of art.

The people and commercial products, on all
The islands of all those far seas,
Have no value, as compared to that value which
    clings
Around sentiments, uplifting, like these;

"The right to govern rests upon the consent
Of the governed," and further that,
"All men are created free and equal,"
In some places disregarded so flat.

Now, it seems to me, that, the highest duty,
Which this nation owes to itself,
And its traditions, is to put the negro of the
    South
On that plane of intelligence, moral health,

And civilization, where no man will be tempted,
Himself to degrade, by interpreting constitution
    to mean
One thing, when applied to a black man,
And another, when to white men.

If ignorance and poverty, of the negro of the
    South,
Is permitted to corrupt and warp laws,
Degrade public conscience, result will be felt
Through acquired territory and all parts of
    the North.

To be willing to defend one's country with
  his life,
You say, is the highest test
Of patriotism, usefulness; offer in strife
To try, duties to perform, each one, his best.

Here you have a race but thirty-five years
Out of slavery; but few hundred removed
From savagery's haunts, battles and fears:
All can see he has greatly improved.

You place the Negro soldier of this race, dark,
On the one hand, by the side of the wealth
And culture of the East; New England, New
    York,
On the other, intelligence, chivalry of the South,

In front of him you place the soldiery of one
Of the oldest, most renowned, of the earth,
A country of Europe; now, Ethiopia's son,
Prove your right as a man; prove your worth.

For answer with a bravery and impetuosity,
That shall live in story and song,
"My Country 'Tis of Thee" flowing from his
  lips,
He scales the heights of San Juan; the battle's won!

Is won for his country, is it won for himself?
Let this serious question employ
The thoughts of humanitarians of wealth,
Bring full justice, rights, all shall enjoy.

At the armory, of the First Infantry, assembled
    a crowd
That filled the immense structure to the door,
Gathered to hear General Shafter, who said
What follows and considerably more:

"There's nothing so dear to the heart of the
    President
Of this Republic, proud, as to know
That he is approved; by the people sustained;
That approval events plainly show.

I accept your welcome, so far as I am concerned
As commander of the army, which, so
Recently, by its successful campaign
Hauled Spain's standard down, laid it low:

The standard which, for four hundred years,
Has floated on this continent;
Never again to be raised here, (applause)
Americans have decreed, their intent.

But in thus recognizing me, I wish you to know
That the credit is not due to me,
For the accomplished results, which now show,
Except in a very small degree.

It is due to the army, my gallant command,
A better in America ne'er stood:
Saying that I'll not apologize to the old army, grand,
These, their sons, are their equals; as good:

They had the advantage at the close of the war
That they had been oft tried by fire,
And practically knew what war was, then, of yore,
What to look for, in dread battles dire.

While perfect in discipline, this army of mine,
Magnificent shots, thoroughly drilled,
Were deficient, only, in that they'd ne'er been
Under fire, where brave hearts are stilled:

And it is to them that credit and thanks
Are due, and I now wish to say,
To their heroism, indomitable will, pluck and strength,
We're indebted for victory, to-day:

For, I tell you, my comrades, that e'en after
    going through
That four years of war, in my youth,
Having with me men who then fought against us,
Also, veterans, who will bear out this truth,

When I say, that, their unanimous voice
Was, that soldiers ne'er suffered before
In American campaign, so severely were tried,
As in this, at Santiago's door."

He then gave an interesting account of the
    campaign,
And the enormous difficulties met;
They were not in the fighting at all, so he said,
For that was the easiest part:

But in getting food and medicine to the front,
Over the single, muddy, terrible road:
Fourteen horses instead of four it took,
The battery was such a great load.

Secretary of Agriculture, Iowa's Wilson, next
    spoke
As follows, save that this is condensed:
"The history of the nations of the old world,
Mainly of wars with each other consists.

Changes of dynasties and of boundaries, too,
In conformance to results of the war;
Religious and civil liberty, through
War with intrenched oppression's bar.

Great campaigns and their decisive battles are
Mountain peaks of records, of the past,
Overshadowing the growth of education, thought
And action; in history they last:

Many of their histories are but chronicles
Of conflicts that brought glory to
The crowned head on one side, to the other, shame,
Humiliation, most painful to view.

The right of succession, there, to a throne,
Has cost hundreds of thousands of lives
Of people who were not interested in result;
Thus power and oppression there thrives:

And the desire to compel all people to conform,
In their devotional exercise,
To the will of somebody, high in power,
The cause, of millions slaughtered, supplies.

The most potent influences in arresting war,
Have been education and growth
Of commerce, between nations, grouping of
    the weak
And the gospel, by evangels set forth.

The war with Spain, for this reason was waged:
The enlightened people of each state,
The inhuman practices on her colonies, by Spain,
At our doors, we could not tolerate.

There was no hope or desire for profit or gain,
Or national aggrandizement:
From beginning, that 'twould be, this war with Spain,
Expensive, 'twas plainly evident.

'Twas plain that disease would our soldiers attack,
Let precautions be however great;
But when duty was placed in the balance, back,
Those considerations carried no weight.

We were not well prepared, but abundance we had
Of population, wealth, unorganized;
Undisciplined courage and patriotism, grand!
Rushed forward and the whole world surprised.

The events of a few months have given us a name
That forever associated will be
With the most brilliant period, also president revered,
Equal to any in our history.

Consider our position, then, in China seas;
When war was declared, did not own
A post, to which we a vessel could moor,
When, on first of May's dawn, the sun shone,

And the laws of neutrality drove Dewey out
Upon the waters, homeless, with his fleet,
American commerce in the Pacific, throughout,
Was then at Spain's mercy complete.

War had been declared and issue been joined
'Tween a nation that nothing e'er learns
And a nation that nothing e'er permits to escape,
Ere sunset, 'twas the whole world's concerns:

When the sun set on the waters of Manila bay,
The American flag floated forth;
The young Republic graduated into the way
And work of great nations of earth.

The nations of the old world standing armies
    support,
While our commonwealths support schools,
The products of both at Santiago met
To compare results, under war's rules.

The Spaniards, highly disciplined and well
    equipped,
Held positions, strongly intrenched,
Which through centuries and precedent of the
    past, they'd held:
Yet were routed by America's strength.

Though Americans equalled not, in number,
    their foes,
They, contending for the rights of mankind,
School house and humanity, before the day's
    close,
Won the victory, and, to peace, all inclined:

And responsibility, there surrendered by Spain,
Falls, now, upon the United States,
Will be met and discharged with increasing
    gain
To inhabitants inside their gates.

Those islands will get enterprise, good laws,
School houses, capital, and skill,
Honest levying, collecting for expense, in each
    cause
Drop bitterness, be of good cheer and, will.

When God has a work to be done, in this world—
And He has much to do—He prepares
His agents to carry out, perfectly, His will,
Thus our people He has fully endowed.

The cries of the people of Carribean Isles
And China seas entered His ear,
So He put in the hearts of our people erstwhiles
As Samaritans to come forth, interfere.

Many years intervened before we could see
Our strong obligations to Him,
Responsibility to our God to be
As it was, all throughout interim.

The finger of Providence all recognize
In many incidents of the war;
The navy lost few men in conflict or by disease,
Not a ship lost, although they sailed far.

The transportation and landing of troops,
At Cuba, Manila, Porto Rico,
Were surprises in their exemption from disaster;
Never before was such record to show.

We suffered more in camp than in battle;
Moses, over three thousand years ago,
Told how to behave in camp, in plain detail,
In the Bible's safe reading 'twill show,

God turned the shot aside from each fleet
And held the dread cyclone in hand,
'Till landing and victories, both, were complete;
Then came storms, in fury o'er, the land.

The war cost, directly, three hundred million
    dollars,
But the expenditure is less cause for regret
Than the loss of one of our soldiers
Who has died, in battle or camp, yet.

In 1879, one hundred millions in gold
In the treasury we put to take care
Of our credit, our nation, staunch, to uphold,
Now the same put in battleships, rare.

Is alarm felt at probable use of these ships?
Let us from a peace standpoint e'er be
Ready, God's will and humanity's cause
To espouse, help, humanity to free.

The vessels may not be used, for many a day,
Otherwise, than our commerce to protect,
But on nations who recognize not man as a man,
They cannot but have good effect.

Let those nations who oppress the common people gaze
And see, there's a nation on earth,
That one billion four hundred million dollars could raise,
And two hundred and fifty thousand men equip in one month.

And that three hundred millions it did expend
Overcoming, for humanity's sakes,
One of oldest, proudest nations on earth did then send
To the rear, for her crimes, and mistakes,

In one hundred and thirteen days: doing God's work;
As, is firmly believed everywhere,
In never an instance did their duty once shirk
Or advantages take, unfair.

A dull student of events he would be who supposed,
That the United States could avoid
Her duties to mankind, by keeping her doors closed
Like a hermit, live unemployed.

The world demands the most competent men
To take charge and manage affairs,
Best machinery, commodities, we're producing
    them
And our flag protects, U. S. so declares.

And mercy, sublimest attribute of God,
Placed above judgment, justice and truth,
We have shown and are showing to even the clod
In man's form, undeserving and ruth.

Monsters of history no mercy have shown,
Governor-General of Philippine Isles
Threatened the lash, and, had he victory won,
His word he'd have kept there, erstwhiles.

Dewey refrained from shelling the town
Out of considerations of mercy, sublime!
Looked the other way, when Governor-General
    stepped down
And, away from Manila, made time.

Throughout this war, for humanity,
Our operations on principles humane,
Were conducted, and our President sought,
    without war,
Perfect justice, satisfaction, to gain.

For necessities, comforts, most lavish expense,
For army and navy, was ne'er spared:
And our sailors at Manila and at Santiago
For all Spanish wounded, there cared.

The Cubans we fed before war began,
During continuance and we're feeding them still:
The American people, rich, poor, every one,
Give of means, time and hearty good will.

To the fever stricken soldiers they gladly give aid,
In every possible way,
Their true heroism, characteristic of people humane,
Is plain to be seen, we must say.

Deeds of daring have challenged, the admiration of the world,
From beginning of conflict till close;
A marvel is the work of Dewey and his men,
In the orient, where the tropic breeze blows.

The performance of Sampson and sailors so bold,
In Carribean seas, glorify
American history, 'twill in pages be told
Long as time, and the stars and stripes fly.

The charges at San Juan and El Caney, grand,
Resemble Gettysburg and Balaklava;
Wheeler, rising from a sick bed, goes with
    his command,
Frail of body, sublime of spirit, heroically!

Recalls the Duke of Luxemburg and the Prince
    of Orange,
Europe's greatest generals in their day:
Both equally heroic and equally frail,
Mental powers, bold and fearless, held away.

The calculating courage of Hobson is the pride
Of every student who sees hope of success;
And Roosevelt exemplifies latent warlike qual-
    ities
Of Americans, without preparation, all confess.

The American people in purpose and sympathy
Have been one for many long years,
Of it, the late war furnishes historic evidence,
So, quieted, now, are all fears.

Lee and Wheeler commanded men from the
    wheat fields of the North,
Miles and Grant, men from the cottonfields
    of the South,
Their loyalty and patriotism showed their true
    worth,
And their praises are in every mouth.

The valor of those who for ideas fought,
As each section understood to be right,
From eighteen sixty to sixty five, brought
Common heritage, now, to all, in clear sight."

Other meetings were held in various parts,
Jubilee services in schools, twenty-four;
At Studebaker Hall, presiding officer; Grosscup,
Speakers; Beveridge, Northrup, Rose, had the floor.

A large crowd of workingmen at armory of the Second,
Where Gompers, of speakers, was chief;
His address against expansion as favoring imperialism,
And the same said he of army's increase.

At North Side Turner Hall, addresses were made
By General Adna R. Chaffee
And Postmaster General, Charles Emory Smith,
At this meeting of Peace Jubilee.

After conclusion of exercises at Auditorium,
The President was at lunch entertained
At the Auditorium Hotel by Jubilee Committeemen:
Meantime, outside, how it rained!

At table with the President, Thos. B. Bryan,
R. J. Oglesby, Judge John Barton Payne,
Captain Lafayette McWilliams, and several ladies
Of the presidential party, not named.

At its close the President left for the Mc-
    Williams home,
Where he rested till departure for the ball,
Where four thousand people danced, at the
    Auditorium,
For the benefit of soldiers, sailors, all.

This Jubilee Ball, was a notable success;
Twenty five thousand dollars the gain:
General Miles, General Chaffee, Shafter and
    the rest
Were there, heroes, all, of this war with Spain.

Chinese and Corean Embassies here,
And dignitaries, most high,
Including forenoon's speakers, Ireland and
    Speer,
And of numberless others supply.

The hour set for reception of distinguished
    guests
Was 10:30, before specified time,
The reception committee, headed by Mrs.
    Palmer,
Attended by Marshall Field, were in line.

Stationed behind ribbons of red, white and blue
That were stretched out, long, 'cross the hall,
To wait for the President, who appeared true
To time, with Chairman Truax, Mayor Harrison, all.

The orchestra, "Star Spangled Banner," then played,
While the throng enthusiastically applaud,
When ceremony of presentation was stayed,
In his box sat the President and bowed.

At 11:30 he visited Medinah Temple,
There the ball of the Naval Reserves;
Several hundred gathered in uniform, full,
These heroes whom nothing e'er swerves.

The President, arm in arm with Mayor Harrison,
Accompanied by McCalla of the Marblehead,
Admiral Brown, Commodore Ide, Capt. Wise, Lieut. W. J. Wilson,
Lieut. J. A. Ubdell, Ensigns; D. R. Colins, S. D. Flood.

They were greeted with cheers most heartily prolonged,
Ten minutes were occupied shaking hands
With the President, filing past whom they thronged,
Then at east the end of hall, he there stands.

Addressing the blue jackets, briefly, he said;
"It gives me great pleasure indeed
To meet the Chicago Naval Reserve,
That magnificent work did, with speed,

At Santiago, where Cervera's fleet
Was destroyed, which to suspension led
Of hostilities, giving us hope, peace to greet,
On justice, right, humanity, founded.

Never did men more gallant in both Army and
    Navy
Muster, to glorious stripes and bright stars,
Than the soldiers and sailors in the late
    Spanish war,
And their victory no blemish e'er mars.

While either ocean's breast bears a white sail,
Your name will men never forget;
While ever God's sun steers each ship through
    the gale,
In remembrance, dear, you'll be held yet."

The President departed amidst the loud cheers
Which ended this grand Jubilee,
Remembered 'twill be for many long years,
Throughout this, "The Land of the Free."

To Our Boys of the 49th and 51st Iowa.

Oh, how the heart swells,
The silent tear tells,
When of patriotism, grand, we read!
How we wish then to do
A courageous act, too,
Or in some great good to take lead.

Oh, will our hearts break
When to Cuba they take
Forty-ninth for a garrison there?
Here's our chance to be brave,
For, Our Boys, first, we gave,
But, "Send them back," now is our prayer.

The Fifty-first, oh,
To Manila must go,
And the poor mothers' hearts ache in vain!
In vain is their prayer,
The boys must go where
They are needed, and sent; that is plain.

And our duty, true,
Is to cheer them, anew,
And confide them to God's loving care.
Oh, our bonnie boys brave,
There is more you must save
Than the body! Of sin, then, beware!

Think of mother and home
And the tempter'll not come;
God will help you to drive him away.
Pure in heart you'll return,
Bright your lamp then will burn,
Lighting others that might go astray.

It is brave to be true,
Keeping heaven in view.
Moral courage is greatest of all.
More firmness it takes,
Doing right for their sakes,
Than required scaling mountain or wall.

You wish great deeds to do,
Here's your chance; just be true
To your God and your country and home;
Scorn the wrong with your might,
It will sneak out of sight
And never back to you will come.

Trust in God for the rest
And then what is best,
Sure, will come: For to him who doth wait
All things come at last:
Hold God's promises fast
And you're safe whatever your fate.

Then as heroes of right,
In all the world's sight,
You'll be greeted with honor and love.
How our proud hearts will swell,
When of "Our Boys" they tell,
"They are heroes recorded above."

Equal to any Occasion . . .

Equal to any occasion
The Iowa boys stand today,
They're the pride of our state and nation,
On all sides, everything goes their way.

At Palo Alto at football
They defeated the Crack Stanford team,
6 to 0, was the score, and all
Cheer them; now let Iowa's bird crow or scream.

Still annother game played at Berkley,
The Fifty-first Iowa boys win
From the University of California,
6 to 0 stands the score again.

At both places were given ovations,
The whole regiment took holiday,
Afterward on drill at Pavilion
They took honors the very same way.

Thus you see our boys bring credit
Our state, Iowa, they represent.
Time and effort spent in home training
All can see now, was time well spent.

And our Iowa home boys, also,
Have done the self same thing,
Have whipped Nebraska at football,
And their victory too, we sing.

Aunt Beckey Young . . .

I've been over to see Aunt Beckey
Oh! isn't it a treat,
To sit in her cosy kitchen
Where every thing's so neat,
And listen while she tells me
Of many things, to me, new;
Her soldier boys, their marches,
And the battles they went through.

During the Civil war she was with them
At hospital, in the field,
After hard fought battles,
Where neither side would yield:
Oh, the dreaded amputations,
The miseries and pains
After each great battle,
No matter which side gains!

As I listen while she tells me,
I feel my heart to swell
And wish I could have done likewise,
Could have gone to front as well,
And I look upon her badges,
Three hundred different kinds,
Representing three hundred lodges,
And more than as many minds,

That invented badges, different,
For each occasion fit;
And Aunt Beckey deserves them every one,
We're very sure of that,
For she went from her home in Ithaca,
New York, in 'sixty-two,
Returned again in 'sixty-five
After the war was through.

During those three years she was every where
With 109th New York,
In which she and her two brothers were,
There, kept up her work
As nurse, in hospital or field
With the Ninth Army Corps,
Army of the Potomac,
'Til the Civil war was o'er.

Came to Iowa in 1868
And since then, Aunt Beckey's found
In patriotic organizations,
Throughout the country 'round.
And all delight to honor
The nurse, who freely gave
Her time and work for nothing,
The soldiers lives to save.

Thus, when this Spanish war broke out.
Her advice was eagerly sought,
In making what was needed
Sanitary Commission brought
Their plans and cares to Aunt Beckey;
With all, she sympathized;
Helped their constant, patriotic work,
In their councils she advised.

Long live our dear Aunt Beckey!
Iowa claims her now,
But as New York was her native state,
To New York we all must bow.
Her father was James Graham,
A soldier of 1812;
His only sister, a nurse with him,
From camp fever, lost her life.

So its plain to be seen, Aunt Beckey
Comes of patriotic stock,
She's true as steel, and patient
And steady as the clock,
To all she's ever ready
To extend a kindly hand.
May heaven watch over Aunt Beckey
Our Boys, and our native land.

Where's My Papa . . .

"Mamma, where's my papa?
Why can't I find him? say,
Was I a teenty baby
When my papa went away?"

"Why did he go to heaven?
I want him; Oh, so bad!
If he had only stayed here
Oh, I would be so glad"

"Other little girls have papas,
And Oh! it makes me cry
When they kiss their little girlies.
Why did my papa die?"

My darling, your papa was a soldier,
And was captured in the war
And starved in the cruel prisons
He never was well, my dear.

And when you, little Birdie, darling,
Were only ten months old,
Your papa was called to leave us
In this world that seems so cold,

To orphan children, who are left here,
But darling you must pray
To "Our Father who art in heaven,"
He can hear every word you say.

So, ask a blessing, baby,
And to us it will be given
That we shall see our papa,
We'll meet him up in heaven.

Sanitary Commission . . .

Iowa's Sanitary Commission, reorganized the 9th
    of May,
Less than one month had war been under way,
When a number of women thinking, the volun-
    teers would need
Many hospital supplies, began sewing, with speed,
In the Y. M. C. A. Building, using library room,
Donated for the purpose, that there they might
    come.

There they worked all summer making housewives
Bandages, pads and other supplies:
And hundreds of sheets, towels and pillow cases,
And nightshirts, too, sent from many places,
To Sanitary Commission, in turn by them sent
To Colonels of each and every Iowa Regiment.

And to Iowa's brave immunes, also, a share,
And still they kept working till they'd supplies
    and to spare;
When the 52d Iowa boys come home, as they ought,
Thirty-eight very sick, to Cottage Hospital were
    brought,
Then everything was needed, all the things sent,
For their comfort, welfare, was much money, well
    spent.

A chain letter had been started, some time in June
Or early in July, not a day too soon.
It went on its mission, to do good it was bound
As it passed from four friends to four other friends 'round;
Then each of these four sent four others the same
Ten cents, from each, to the treasury came.

This blessed chain letter became noted, as well,
Its mission of usefulness let the convalescents tell
How in comfort it kept them, paying each bill,
Many nurses, well paid, and prescriptions did fill,
And other expenses which as high ran
As three hundred dollars per week, led the van,

Of all sources of income it proved itself best
To bring in ready cash and to keep up a zest,
Renewing interest and faith in each move
Of sanitary commission and their labor of love;
Their patriotism, perseverance, self-denial, prove
Christian earnestness; reward rests with heaven above.

Iowa's Soldier Girl . . .

We're interested in Miss Della Weeks,
"Our Iowa Soldier Girl;"
We read and think and talk of her
'Til our heads are in a whirl.
All sorts of questions do we ask,
Not waiting for replies—
How old is she? Where was she born?
What color are her eyes?

She was born November 26, 1864,
In Monroe township, Linn county, Iowa;
With her mother I talked it o'er.
Her father, Charles Weeks, who in 1860
To Linn county came,
Was born in Courtland county, New York, in 1839.
He married Miss Laura Chamberlain in 1862,

Sister of our world-renowned Chamberlains,
Of medicine fame, who
Was born in the same Monroe township
April fifteenth, 'forty-three.
I've answered many questions now,
As you can plainly see.

Miss Della's eyes are black as sloes,
Her hair is thick and dark;
As nurse in hospitals and homes
She succeeded, made her mark,
Visited hospitals of renown
In cities of each state;
To Manilla on St. Paul she's gone,
Out through the golden gate;
To nurse, care for our Iowa boys of the Fifty-first Regiment,
By parents, sisters, wives, sweethearts
And friends, she there was sent.

Osborne Deignan's Welcome Home.

Osborne Deignan, "Our Sailor Boy!"
Proudly we welcome him home, with joy;
No honors can be too great for him;
All lustres beside his name grow dim.

Our Iowa hero! Mortal man
Must pause, his deed of bravery scan;
Immortal is his name, for aye
With Hobson's, none will ask us why.

For dark as Egypt was the night,
Beneath were mines quite out of sight,
When, Deignan, calm,, his hand on helm
Of Merrimac, water must o'erwhelm,

With Claussen, Montague, George Charette,
John Murphy, now of crew of Celt,
George Phillips, now of Vermont's crew,
Frank Kelley, now on on Vermont, too,

Sailed in Santiago's harbor to a doom
Most terrible, it seemed must come
To daring band, so nobly brave,
But, God, above, their lives could save.

All at once Egyptian night,
By constant flash of guns, was light,
And down they kept below the rail,
Or they'd been targets, without fail.

The sea began to churn and foam;
Discovery then they knew had come,
For shot and shell around them fell,
Helpless the ship, in veritable hell.

Forty minutes floated about,
Then sank, in water cast them out,
But not before each touched the mine
Planned to be fired at proper time.

To the catamaran raft they clung,
'Twas for that purpose brought along;
'Mid rifles crack and cannons roar
The night of peril passed, was o'er.

At six o'clock, in morning light,
Admiral Cervera saw their plight,
Took them on shipboard, gave them food,
Treated them as civilized being should.

And now we welcome home "Our Boy,"
Full hearts o'erflowing, each with joy,
But words are lacking to express
Our pride in him, and thankfulness.

That to his home he now has come,
His friends, now greet, with fife and drum
And banners gay, and flags in air,
Their hero, Iowa's hero, there.

And now the "A la Hobson kiss,"
It seems, is not at all amiss;
One hundred maidens demand this;
A measure of his gallantry;

But mother claims the nearest place,
And greets her boy first, face to face,
Tears dim his eyes, 'tis manly grace,
With kisses for mother, deferentially.

The mother's heart is full, we know,
That, God her hero saved to show
His power: Her bliss doth cup o'erflow,
All join in thanks reverentially.

Admonition . . .

"The wages of sin is death,"
Of your morals, "boys," take care;
Keep your hearts pure as the morning breath
Of wind, and free as air.

If you lift your hearts in prayer
To God in time of need;
You'll resist temptation, there
Satan leaves you with all speed.

Much ill-health you can avoid,
Pure in heart you can return,
If your thoughts are well employed—
Let great thoughts within you burn,

Your homes and mother's love,
And sweethearts, pure and good;
Put your trust in God above,
And behave as heroes should.

Repulse each evil thing
That comes before your eyes;
Satan will take to wing,
Away from you he flies.

Your affections keep clean and pure,
Don't flatter and make believe;
'Twill cause you trouble, be sure—
Some heart 'twill sorely grieve.

Only a Flirtation . . .

Only a little flirtation
With a Cuban girl, you say;
Such as most soldiers indulge in,
To while the dull time away.

But, oh! the true heart beating
Under the bodice light,
Never once thought of your cheating
Her, out of life, love and light.

So when at length you sickened,
And to your home were sent,
Her heart-throbs, true, were quickened
To follow you bound; so she went,

Crossed the gulf to the city of Orleans,
From there made her way to your home
In far off South Dakotah,
To nurse you she has come;

When, hearing of preparations
For your marriage, her poor racked brain
Gives way, her heart is broken,
And a madhouse is all her gain.

And you, thoughtless boy, now seeing
Naught but endless troubles to come,
Went out into wild wastes fleeing,
And dead you are brought home.

Oh! will not this story teach you,
Boys, to keep honor in view,
And ne'er to indulge in flirtation,
To your own friends at home be true?

Or, if you had no sweetheart
When you left your home for war,
To be true to one you've since chosen,
And not her entire life mar?

'Tis a crime, my boy, dishonor,
In your uniform bright to shine,
Take advantage of admiration
For heroes in every clime;

Thus pretend, act a lie, say you love her,
Win affections that never can die,
Blot out the heaven above her—
It is seen by God's almighty eye.

Love . . .

The mind's eye may see clearly,
Unwelcome though the fact,
That love may be a hindrance,
Denying power to act
    Worth doing.

But oftener love's a stimulus
That leads one on to fame,
Showing the beloved object
That one can win a name
    Worth having.

Try, build a castle bravely,
And rear its turrets high,
Yes, fashion all in beauty,
Its minarets reach the sky—
    Worth giving

To a most radiant angel
From God's fair climes above;
It is mere nothing, worthless,
Without the boon of Love
    Can greet it.

Moontime Musings . . .

"Every one has his hardships"
'Tis said, let's see if its true:
Let's put our heads together
And of notes compare a few.

You view things from your standpoint,
I will also view from mine,
That of a country schoolma'am:
You say, that's not in your line?

Well if it's not and you're tired
And not inclined to contend
For merits of the saying,
We will not, let's drop it, friend;

Instead let's count the blessings
And beauties around us spread,
O'er paths that teachers travel
In earning their daily bread.

In winter time, for instance,
We wade through beautiful snow,
Breaking the road for others,
For at half past seven we go:

Oh, smooth unbroken surface,
'Tis purer than rays of light!
Even weeds by the roadside,
Now dressed in their robes of white,

Extend their arms out toward us,
In grotesque and varied form,
As trudging through the snowdrifts,
The exertion keeps us warm:

Each side of road are willows
Bent down with their load of sheen,
A coat of mail inclosed in,
Surpassing their summer's green.

Thousands of brightest diamonds
All strung together with care,
Silver filagree workings,
And bright frescoes rich and rare,

Could not compare to beauties,
Here spread out before our eyes:
Nature's fathomless background,
The blue of the heavenly skies.

Thus, after storm comes sunshine,
And after sorrow comes joy,
And after earthly trials
Comes peace, pure, without alloy.

If we can do our duty
And struggle on, bravely, through,
Remember, build for future,
And the good we ought to do,

Sometime there'll be a balance
Of accounts, for teachers, all,
And oh! we hope to merit
And to hear that gracious call,

Come higher, over small things,
Thou hast been faithful found:
Hast used thy humble talents,
And not hid them in the ground.

Ah, then there'll be no hardships!
For all will be overcome,
And oh, how sweet will rest be,
In our last, eternal home.

Weary heart craves sympathy,
And the tired brain wants rest,
There, there alone, we'll find them,
In that haven for the blest.

Tribute to the Soldiers Friend . .

Mrs. Louise Ritchey McKay
Is true to the soldiers alway;
From beginning to end
Their steadfast friend
Is Mrs. Dr. McKay.

Her receptions at each different place,
That both beauty and chivalry grace,
With presence so bright,
Making time's happy flight,
Like a beauteous dream
Or a rippling stream,
Leave a picture which naught can efface.

These attentions, not thrown away,
Will be shrined in sweet memory;
And in future days
Will elicit much praise,
For kindness shown
To these boys, our own,
By Des Moines and Mrs. McKay.

In Conclusion . . .

Our President, McKinley, grand,
Unflinching, firm; his native land
Is honored by his matchless fame,
She gains new lustre by the same.

Detraction could not take away
Or even dull it, for a day;
More bright it shines now victory's won,
Than splendors of the noonday sun.

In wee small hours, in secret prayer,
He draws his inspiration, where
Immortal Lincoln did the same,
And triumphs in Jehovah's name.

In emergency it is the case,
A man is found to fill the place;
A noble illustration, too,
We have in Governor Shaw, so true.

Since war broke out, both day and night,
He's kept the good of all in sight,
And everything the "boys" could need,
He's ordered promptly done with speed.

Our Adjutant, General Byers, too,
Has squarely stood by Boys in Blue,
And firmly taken every care
To have each soldier get his share.

Sanitary Commission, kind,
Have ever kept our boys in mind;
Have worked and prayed and done their best,
That soldiers, sick, might have sweet rest.

The Iowa Red Cross comes, too,
To front in help for Boys in Blue;
God sees all done, and in His Heaven,
Credit to all, reward is given.

Iowa's citizens, one and all,
Respond to each and every call;
Enough for soldiers they can't do
To suit them. Now my story's through.

Our boys that could be spared are home,
God grant the others soon can come
In honor, with each duty clear,
And fully done, we have no fear.

To Mrs. McKay, "The Soldiers' Friend,"
A tribute they most gladly send,
Their thanks, for all so kindly done,
To make Thanksgiving "A Welcome Home!"

www.ingramcontent.com/pod-product-compliance
Lightning Source LLC
Chambersburg PA
CBHW022136160426
43197CB00009B/1313